START
AMAZON WEB SERVICES

Learn Amazon Web Services from the Scratch and
Become a Cloud Guru

Cloud Gurus

Table of Contents

TRAINING SUMMARY

AWS (Amazon Web Service) is a cloud computing platform that enables users to access on demand computing services like database storage, virtual cloud server, etc. This online course will give an in-depth knowledge on EC2 instance as well as useful strategy on how to build and modify instance for your own applications.

WHAT SHOULD I KNOW?

This guide is designed for complete beginners. Basic knowledge on cloud computing, networking, storage, security, will be an additional help.

SYLLABUS

- What is AWS? Amazon Cloud Services Tutorial
- How to Create EC2 Instance in AWS: Step by Step Tutorial
- Change Instance Type, Security Group, Termination Protection: AWS EC2
- What is AWS Lambda? Lambda Function with Examples
- AWS Certification Guide: Cost, Courses, Salary, Exam Details
- Azure vs. AWS: Key Differences
- Heroku vs AWS: 10 Most Important Differences You Must Know!
- Digitalocean vs AWS: 10 Most Important Differences You Must Know!
- Google Cloud vs AWS
- 20 BEST AWS Competitors & Alternatives.

WHAT IS AWS?
AMAZON CLOUD SERVICES TUTORIAL

WHAT IS CLOUD COMPUTING?

Cloud computing *is* a term referred to storing and accessing data over the internet. It doesn't store any data on the hard disk of your personal computer. In cloud computing, you can access data from a remote server.

WHAT IS AWS?

Amazon web service is a platform that offers flexible, reliable, scalable, easy-to-use and cost-effective cloud computing solutions.

AWS is a comprehensive, easy to use computing platform offered Amazon. The platform is developed with a combination of infrastructure as a service (IaaS), platform as a service (PaaS) and packaged software as a service (SaaS) offerings.

In this tutorial, you will learn,

- What is Cloud Computing?

- What is AWS?

- History of AWS

- Important AWS Services

- Applications of AWS services

- Companies using AWS

- Advantages of AWS

- Disadvantages of AWS

- Best practices of AWS

HISTORY OF AWS

- 2002- AWS services launched

- 2006- Launched its cloud products

- 2012- Holds first customer event

- 2015- Reveals revenues achieved of $4.6 billion

- 2016- Surpassed $10 billon revenue target

- 2016- Release snowball and snowmobile

- 2019- Offers nearly 100 cloud services

IMPORTANT AWS SERVICES

Amazon Web Services offers a wide range of different business purpose global cloud-based products. The products include storage, databases, analytics, networking, mobile, development tools, enterprise applications, with a pay-as-you-go pricing model.

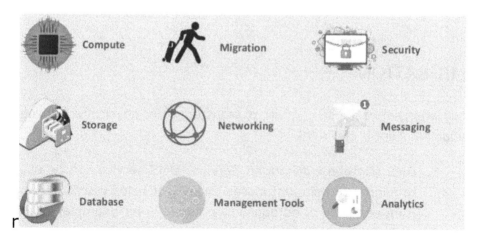

Important AWS Services

Here, are essential AWS services.

AWS COMPUTE SERVICES

Here, are Cloud Compute Services offered by Amazon:

1. EC2(Elastic Compute Cloud) - EC2 is a virtual machine in the cloud on which you have OS level control. You can run this cloud server whenever you want.

2. LightSail-This cloud computing tool automatically deploys and manages the computer, storage, and networking capabilities required to run your applications.

3. Elastic Beanstalk— The tool offers automated deployment and provisioning of resources like a highly scalable production website.

4. EKS (Elastic Container Service for Kubernetes)—The tool allows you toKubernetes on Amazon cloud environment without installation.

5. AWS Lambda—This AWS service allows you to run functions in the cloud. The tool is a big cost saver for you as you to pay only when your functions execute.

MIGRATION

Migration services use   d to transfer data physically between your datacenter and AWS.

1. DMS (Database Migration Service)-DMS service can be used to migrate on-site databases to AWS. It helps you to migrate from one type of database to another — for example, Oracle to MySQL.

2. SMS (Server Migration Service)-SMS migration services allows you to migrate on-site servers to AWS easily and quickly.

3. Snowball—Snowball is a small application which allows you to transfer terabytes of data inside and outside of AWS environment.

STORAGE

1. Amazon Glacier- It is an extremely low-cost storage service. It offers secure and fast storage for data archiving and backup.

2. Amazon Elastic Block Store (EBS)- It provides block-level storage to use with Amazon EC2 instances. Amazon Elastic Block Store volumes are network-attached and remain independent from the life of an instance.

3. AWS Storage Gateway- This AWS service is connecting on-premises software applications with cloud-based storage. 10It offers secure integration between the company's on-premises and AWS's storage infrastructure.

SECURITY SERVICES

1. IAM (Identity and Access Management)— IAM is a secure cloud security service which helps you to manage users, assign policies, form groups to manage multiple users.

2. Inspector—It is an agent that you can install on your virtual machines, which reports any security vulnerabilities.

3. Certificate Manager—The service offers free SSL certificates for your domains that are managed by Route53.

4. WAF (Web Application Firewall)— WAF security service offers application-level protection and allows you to block SQL injection and helps you to block cross-site scripting attacks.

5. Cloud Directory—This service allows you to create flexible, cloud-native directories for managing hierarchies of data along multiple dimensions.

6. KMS (Key Management Service)—It is a managed service. This security service helps you to create and control the encryption keys which allows you to encrypt your data.

7. Organizations—You can create groups of AWS accounts using this service to manages security and automation settings.

8. Shield—Shield is managed DDoS (Distributed Denial of Service protection service). It offers safeguards against web applications running on AWS.

9. Macie—It offers a data visibility security service which helps classify and protect your sensitive critical content.

10. GuardDuty —It offers threat detection to protect your AWS accounts and workloads.

DATABASE SERVICES

1. Amazon RDS- This Database AWS service is easy to set up, operate, and scale a relational database in the cloud.

2. Amazon DynamoDB- It is a fast, fully managed NoSQL database service. It is a simple service which allow cost-effective storage and retrieval of data. It also allows you to serve any level of request traffic.

3. Amazon ElastiCache- It is a web service which makes it easy to deploy, operate, and scale an in-memory cache in the cloud.

4. Neptune- It is a fast, reliable and scalable graph database service.

5. Amazon RedShift-It is Amazon's data warehousing solution which you can use to perform complex OLAP queries.

ANALYTICS

1. Athena—This analytics service allows perm SQL queries on your S3 bucket to find files.

2. CloudSearch—You should use this AWS service to create a fully managed search engine for your website.

3. ElasticSearch—It is similar to CloudSearch. However, it offers more features like application monitoring.

4. Kinesis—This AWS analytics service helps you to stream and analyzing real-time data at massive scale.

5. QuickSight —It is a business analytics tool. It helps you to create visualizations in a dashboard for data in Amazon Web Services. For example, S3, DynamoDB, etc.

6. EMR (Elastic Map Reduce)—This AWS analytics service mainly used for big data processing like Spark, Splunk, Hadoop, etc.

7. Data Pipeline—Allows you to move data from one place to another. For example from DynamoDB to S3.

MANAGEMENT SERVICES

1. CloudWatch—Cloud watch helps you to monitor AWS environments like EC2, RDS instances, and CPU utilization. It also triggers alarms depends on various metrics.

2. CloudFormation—It is a way of turning infrastructure into the cloud. You can use templates for providing a whole production environment in minutes.

3. CloudTrail—It offers an easy method of auditing AWS resources. It helps you to log all changes.

4. OpsWorks—The service allows you to automated Chef/Puppet deployments on AWS environment.

5. Config—This AWS service monitors your environment. The tool sends alerts about changes when you break certain defined configurations.

6. Service Catalog—This service helps large enterprises to authorize which services user will be used and which won't.

7. AWS Auto Scaling—The service allows you to automatically scale your resources up and down based on given CloudWatch metrics.

8. Systems Manager—This AWS service allows you to group your resources. It allows you to identify issues and act on them.

9. Managed Services—It offers management of your AWS infrastructure which allows you to focus on your applications.

INTERNET OF THINGS

1. IoT Core— It is a managed cloud AWS service. The service allows connected deviceslike cars, light bulbs, sensor grids, to securely interact with cloud applications and other devices.

2. IoT Device Management—It allows you to manage your IoT devices at any scale.

3. IoT Analytics—This AWS IOT service is helpful to perform analysis on data collected by your IoT devices.

4. Amazon FreeRTOS—This real-time operating system for microcontrollers helps you to connect IoT devices in the local server or into the cloud.

APPLICATION SERVICES

1. Step Functions—It is a way of visualizing what's going inside your application and what different microservices it is using.

2. SWF (Simple Workflow Service)—The service helps you to coordinate both automated tasks and human-led tasks.

3. SNS (Simple Notification Service)—You can use this service to send you notifications in the form of email and SMS based on given AWS services.

4. SQS (Simple Queue Service)—Use this AWS service to decouple your applications. It is a pull-based service.

5. Elastic Transcoder—This AWS service tool helps you to changes a video's format and resolution to support various devices like tablets, smartphones, and laptops of different resolutions.

DEPLOYMENT AND MANAGEMENT

1. AWS CloudTrail: The services records AWS API calls and send backlog files to you.

2. Amazon CloudWatch: The tools monitor AWS resources like Amazon EC2 and Amazon RDS DB Instances. It also allows you to monitor custom metrics created by user's applications and services.

3. AWS CloudHSM: This AWS service helps you meet corporate, regulatory, and contractual, compliance requirements for maintaining data security by using the Hardware Security Module(HSM) appliances inside the AWS environment.

DEVELOPER TOOLS

1. CodeStar—Codestar is a cloud-based service for creating, managing, and working with various software development projects on AWS.

2. CodeCommit— It is AWS's version control service which allows you to store your code and other assets privately in the cloud.

3. CodeBuild—This Amazon developer service help you to automates the process of building and compiling your code.

4. CodeDeploy—It is a way of deploying your code in EC2 instances automatically.

5. CodePipeline—It helps you create a deployment pipeline like testing, building, testing, authentication, deployment on development and production environments.

6. Cloud9 —It is an Integrated Development Environment for writing, running, and debugging code in the cloud.

MOBILE SERVICES

1. Mobile Hub—Allows you to add, configure and design features for mobile apps.

2. Cognito—Allows users to signup using his or her social identity.

3. Device Farm—Device farm helps you to improve the quality of apps by quickly testing hundreds of mobile devices.

4. AWS AppSync —It is a fully managed GraphQL service that offers real-time data synchronization and offline programming features.

BUSINESS PRODUCTIVITY

1. Alexa for Business—It empowers your organization with voice, using Alexa. It will help you to Allows you to build custom voice skills for your organization.

2. Chime—Can be used for online meeting and video conferencing.

3. WorkDocs—Helps to store documents in the cloud

4. WorkMail—Allows you to send and receive business emails.

DESKTOP & APP STREAMING

1. WorkSpaces—Workspace is a VDI (Virtual Desktop Infrastructure). It allows you to use remote desktops in the cloud.

2. AppStream —A way of streaming desktop applications to your users in the web browser. For example, using MS Word in Google Chrome.

ARTIFICIAL INTELLIGENCE

1. Lex—Lex tool helps you to build chatbots quickly.

2. Polly—It is AWS's text-to-speech service allows you to create audio versions of your notes.

3. Rekognition —It is AWS's face recognition service. This AWS service helps you to recognize faces and object in images and videos.

4. SageMaker—Sagemaker allows you to build, train, and deploy machine learning models at any scale.

5. Transcribe—It is AWS's speech-to-text service that offers high-quality and affordable transcriptions.

6. Translate—It is a very similar tool to Google Translate which allows you to translate text in one language to another.

AR & VR (AUGMENTED REALITY & VIRTUAL REALITY)

Sumerian—Sumerian is a set of tool for offering high-quality virtual reality (VR) experiences on the web. The service allows you to create interactive 3D scenes and publish it as a website for users to access.

CUSTOMER ENGAGEMENT

1. Amazon Connect—Amazon Connect allows you to create your customer care center in the cloud.

2. Pinpoint—Pinpoint helps you to understand your users and engage with them.

3. SES (Simple Email Service)—Helps you to send bulk emails to your customers at a relatively cost-effective price.

GAME DEVELOPMENT

GameLift- It is a service which is managed by AWS. You can use this service to host dedicated game servers. It allows you to scale seamlessly without taking your game offline.

APPLICATIONS OF AWS SERVICES

Amazon Web services are widely used for various computing purposes like:

- Web site hosting
- Application hosting/SaaS hosting
- Media Sharing (Image/ Video)
- Mobile and Social Applications
- Content delivery and Media Distribution

- Storage, backup, and disaster recovery
- Development and test environments
- Academic Computing
- Search Engines
- Social Networking

COMPANIES USING AWS

- Instagram
- Zoopla
- Smugmug
- Pinterest
- Netflix
- Dropbox
- Etsy
- Talkbox
- Playfish
- Ftopia

ADVANTAGES OF AWS

Following are the pros of using AWS services:

- AWS allows organizations to use the already familiar programming models, operating systems, databases, and architectures.
- It is a cost-effective service that allows you to pay only for what you use, without any up-front or long-term commitments.
- You will not require to spend money on running and maintaining data centers.
- Offers fast deployments
- You can easily add or remove capacity.
- You are allowed cloud access quickly with limitless capacity.
- Total Cost of Ownership is very low compared to any private/dedicated servers.
- Offers Centralized Billing and management
- Offers Hybrid Capabilities
- Allows you to deploy your application in multiple regions around the world with just a few clicks

DISADVANTAGES OF AWS

- If you need more immediate or intensive assistance, you'll have to opt for paid support packages.

- Amazon Web Services may have some common cloud computing issues when you move to a cloud. For example, downtime, limited control, and backup protection.

- AWS sets default limits on resources which differ from region to region. These resources consist of images, volumes, and snapshots.

- Hardware-level changes happen to your application which may not offer the best performance and usage of your applications.

BEST PRACTICES OF AWS

- You need to design for failure, but nothing will fail.

- It's important to decouple all your components before using AWS services.

- You need to keep dynamic data closer to compute and static data closer to the user.

- It's important to know security and performance tradeoffs.

- Pay for computing capacity by the hourly payment method.

- Make a habit of a one-time payment for each instance you want to reserve and to receive a significant discount on the hourly charge.

HOW TO CREATE EC2 INSTANCE IN AWS: STEP BY STEP TUTORIAL

WHAT IS AMAZON EC2 INSTANCE?

An EC2 instance is nothing but a virtual server in Amazon Web services terminology. It stands for Elastic Compute Cloud. It is a web service where an AWS subscriber can request and provision a compute server in AWS cloud.

An on-demand EC2 instance is an offering from AWS where the subscriber/user can rent the virtual server per hour and use it to deploy his/her own applications.

The instance will be charged per hour with different rates based on the type of the instance chosen. AWS provides multiple instance types for the respective business needs of the user.

Thus, you can rent an instance based on your own CPU and memory requirements and use it as long as you want. You can terminate the instance when it's no more used and save on costs. This is the most striking advantage of an on-demand instance- you can drastically save on your CAPEX.

In this tutorial, you will learn-

- Login and access to AWS services
- Choose AMI
- Choose EC2 Instance Types
- Configure Instance
- Add Storage
- Tag Instance
- Configure Security Groups
- Review Instances
- Create a EIP and connect to your instance

- What is Spot Instance?
- Create a Spot Request
- Find Instance Types
- Configure the Spot instance
- Review your Spot instance

Let us see in detail how to launch an on-demand EC2 instance in AWS Cloud.

LOGIN AND ACCESS TO AWS SERVICES

Step 1) In this step,

Login to your AWS account and go to the AWS Services tab at the top left corner.

Here, you will see all of the AWS Services categorized as per their area viz. Compute, Storage, Database, etc. For creating an EC2 instance, we have to choose Compute EC2 as in the next step.

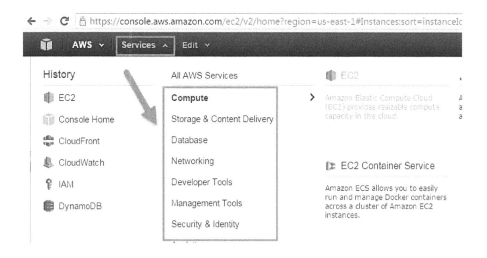

Open all the services and click on EC2 under Compute services. This will launch the dashboard of EC2.

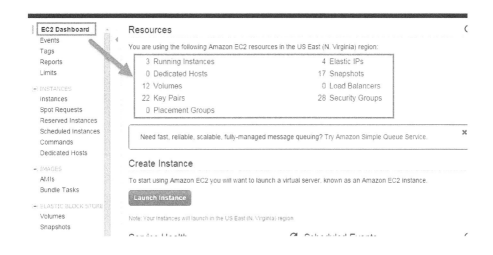

Step 2) On the top right corner of the EC2 dashboard, choose the AWS Region in which you want to provision the EC2 server.

Here we are selecting N. Virginia. AWS provides 10 Regions all over the globe.

Step 3) In this step

Once your desired Region is selected, come back to the EC2 Dashboard.

Click on 'Launch Instance' button in the section of Create Instance (as shown below).

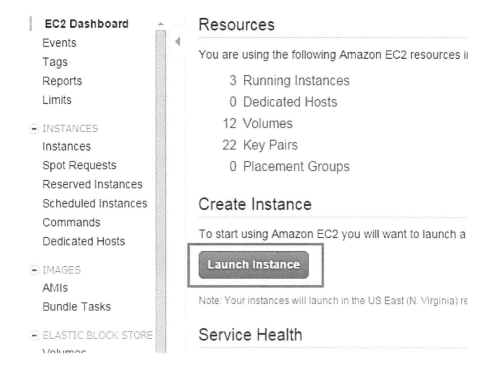

Instance creation wizard page will open as soon as you click 'Launch Instance'.

CHOOSE AMI

In this step we will do,

You will be asked to choose an AMI of your choice. (An AMI is an Amazon Machine Image. It is a template basically of an Operating System platform which you can use as a base to create your instance). Once you launch an EC2 instance from your preferred AMI, the instance will automatically be booted with the desired OS. (We will see more about AMIs in the coming part of the tutorial).

Here we are choosing the default Amazon Linux (64 bit) AMI.

CHOOSE EC2 INSTANCE TYPES

In the next step, you have to choose the type of instance you require based on your business needs.

We will choose t2.micro instance type, which is a 1vCPU and 1GB memory server offered by AWS.

Click on "Configure Instance Details" for further configurations

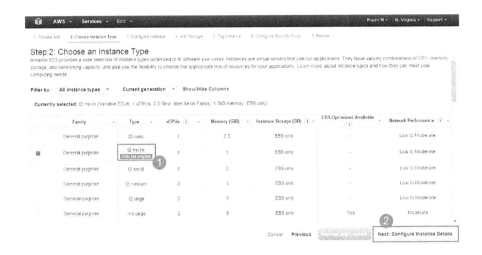

In the next step of the wizard, enter details like no. of instances you want to launch at a time.

Here we are launching one instance.

CONFIGURE INSTANCE

Step 1) No. of instances- you can provision up to 20 instances at a time. Here we are launching one instance.

Step 2) Under Purchasing Options, keep the option of 'Request Spot Instances' unchecked as of now. (This is done when we wish to

launch Spot instances instead of on-demand ones. We will come back to Spot instances in the later part of the tutorial).

Step 3) Next, we have to configure some basic networking details for our EC2 server.

You have to decide here, in which VPC (Virtual Private Cloud) you want to launch your instance and under which subnets inside your VPC. It is better to determine and plan this prior to launching the instance. Your AWS architecture set-up should include IP ranges for your subnets etc. pre-planned for better management. (We will see how to create a new VPC in Networking section of the tutorial.

Subnetting should also be pre-planned. E.g.: If it's a web server you should place it in the public subnet and if it's a DB server, you should place it in a private subnet all inside your VPC.

Below,

1. Network section will give a list of VPCs available in our platform.

2. Select an already existing VPC

3. You can also create a new VPC

Here I have selected an already existing VPC where I want to launch my instance.

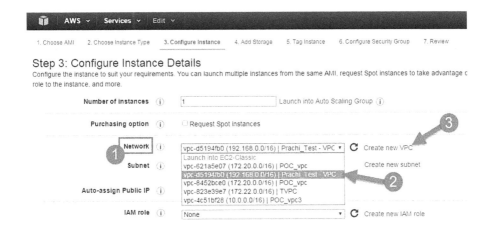

Step 4) In this step,

A VPC consists of subnets, which are IP ranges that are separated for restricting access.

1. Under Subnets, you can choose the subnet where you want to place your instance.

2. I have chosen an already existing public subnet.

3. You can also create a new subnet in this step.

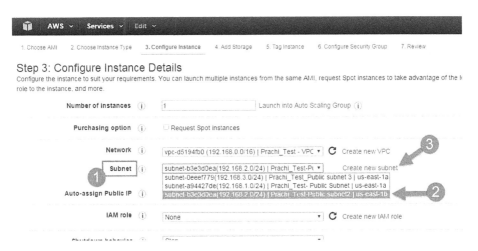

Once your instance is launched in a public subnet, AWS will assign a dynamic public IP to it from their pool of IPs.

Step 5) In this step,

You can choose if you want AWS to assign it an IP automatically, or you want to do it manually later. You can enable/ disable 'Auto assign Public IP' feature here likewise.

Here we are going to assign this instance a static IP called as EIP (Elastic IP) later. So we keep this feature disabled as of now.

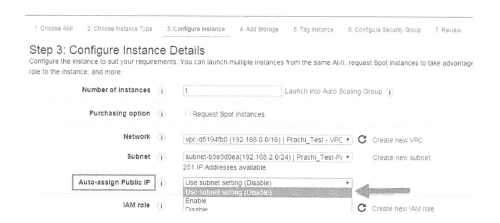

Step 6) In this step,

In the following step, keep the option of IAM role 'None' as of now. We will visit the topic of IAM role in detail in IAM services.

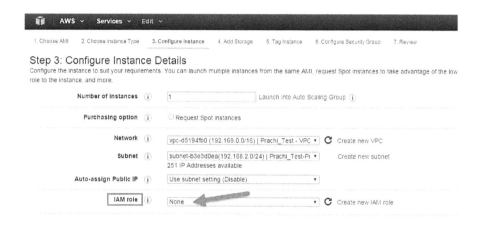

Step 7) In this step, you have to do following things

Shutdown Behavior – when you accidently shut down your instance, you surely don't want it to be deleted but stopped.

Here we are defining my shutdown behavior as Stop.

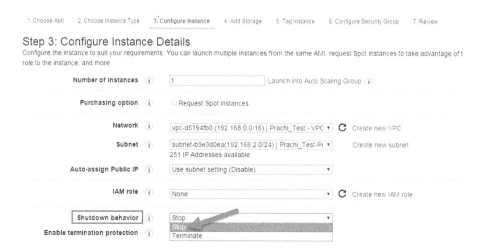

Step 8) In this step,

In case, you have accidently terminated your instance, AWS has a layer of security mechanism. It will not delete your instance if you have enabled accidental termination protection.

Here we are checking the option for further protecting our instance from accidental termination.

Step 9) In this step,

Under Monitoring- you can enable Detailed Monitoring if your instance is a business critical instance. Here we have kept the option unchecked. AWS will always provide Basic monitoring on your instance free of cost. We will visit the topic of monitoring in AWS Cloud Watch part of the tutorial.

Under Tenancy- select the option if shared tenancy. If your application is a highly secure application, then you should go for dedicated capacity. AWS provides both options.

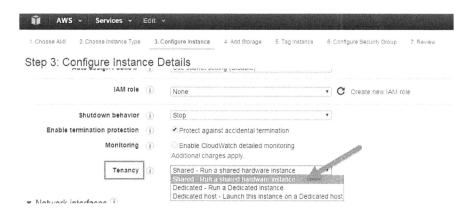

Step 10) In this step,

Click on 'Add Storage' to add data volumes to your instance in next step.

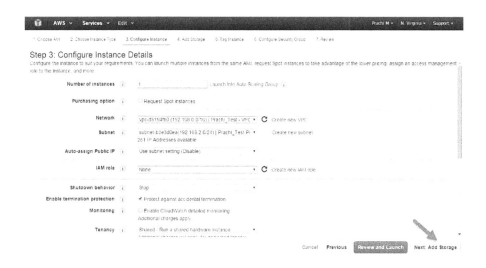

ADD STORAGE

In this step we do following things,

In the Add Storage step, you'll see that the instance has been automatically provisioned a General Purpose SSD root volume of 8GB. (Maximum volume size we can give to a General Purpose volume is 16GB)

You can change your volume size, add new volumes, change the volume type, etc.

AWS provides 3 types of EBS volumes- Magnetic, General Purpose SSD, Provisioned IOPs. You can choose a volume type based on your application's IOPs needs.

TAG INSTANCE

Step 1) In this step

you can tag your instance with a key-value pair. This gives visibility to the AWS account administrator when there are lot number of instances.

The instances should be tagged based on their department, environment like Dev/SIT/Prod. Etc. this gives a clear view of the costing on the instances under one common tag.

1. Here we have tagged the instance as a Dev_Web server 01

2. Go to configure Security Groups later

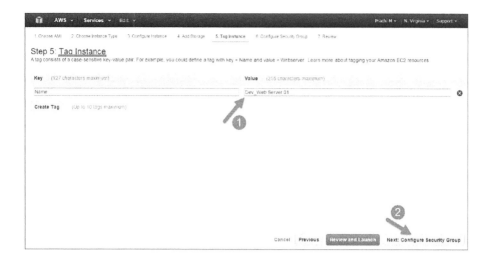

CONFIGURE SECURITY GROUPS

Step 1) In this next step of configuring Security Groups, you can restrict traffic on your instance ports. This is an added firewall mechanism provided by AWS apart from your instance's OS firewall.

You can define open ports and IPs.

Since our server is a webserver=, we will do following things

1. Creating a new Security Group

2. Naming our SG for easier reference

3. Defining protocols which we want enabled on my instance

4. Assigning IPs which are allowed to access our instance on the said protocols

5. Once, the firewall rules are set- Review and launch

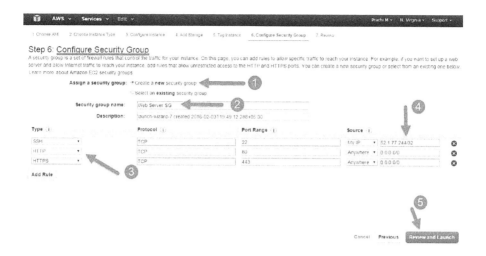

REVIEW INSTANCES

Step 1) In this step, we will review all our choices and parameters and go ahead to launch our instance.

Step 2) In the next step you will be asked to create a key pair to login to you an instance. A key pair is a set of public-private keys.

AWS stores the private key in the instance, and you are asked to download the public key. Make sure you download the key and keep it safe and secured; if it is lost you cannot download it again.

1. Create a new key pair

2. Give a name to your key

3. Download and save it in your secured folder

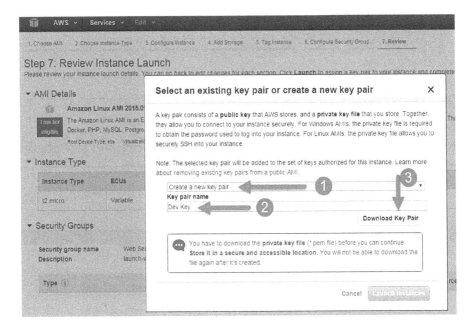

When you download your key, you can open and have a look at your RSA private key.

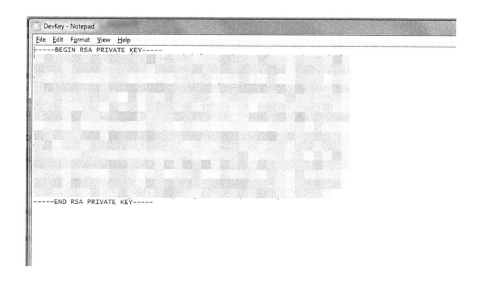

Step 3) Once you are done downloading and saving your key, launch your instance.

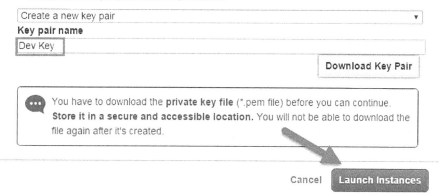

Select an existing key pair or create a new key pair   ✕

A key pair consists of a **public key** that AWS stores, and a **private key file** that you store. Together, they allow you to connect to your instance securely. For Windows AMIs, the private key file is required to obtain the password used to log into your instance. For Linux AMIs, the private key file allows you to securely SSH into your instance.

Note: The selected key pair will be added to the set of keys authorized for this instance. Learn more about removing existing key pairs from a public AMI.

| Create a new key pair | ▼ |

Key pair name

| Dev Key |

Download Key Pair

⦿ You have to download the **private key file** (*.pem file) before you can continue.
Store it in a secure and accessible location. You will not be able to download the file again after it's created.

Cancel   **Launch Instances**

You can see the launch status meanwhile.

Launch Status

Initiating Instance Launches

Please do not close your browser while this is loading

Creating security groups... Successful

Authorizing inbound rules...

You can also see the launch log.

Launch Status

✅ Your instances are now launching
The following instance launches have been initiated: i-4c2c3cff   Hide launch log

Creating security groups	Successful (sg-62d7d21b)
Authorizing inbound rules	Successful
Initiating launches	Successful
Applying tags	Successful

Launch initiation complete

ℹ Get notified of estimated charges
Create billing alerts to get an email notification when estimated charges on your AWS bill exceed an am

Click on the 'Instances' option on the left pane where you can see the status of the instance as 'Pending' for a brief while.

Once your instance is up and running, you can see its status as 'Running' now.

Note that the instance has received a Private IP from the pool of AWS.

CREATE AN EIP AND CONNECT TO YOUR INSTANCE

An EIP is a static public IP provided by AWS. It stands for Elastic IP. Normally when you create an instance, it will receive a public IP from the AWS's pool automatically. If you stop/reboot your instance, this public IP will change- it'dynamic. In order for your application to have a static IP from where you can connect via public networks, you can use an EIP.

Step 1) On the left pane of EC2 Dashboard, you can go to 'Elastic IPs' as shown below.

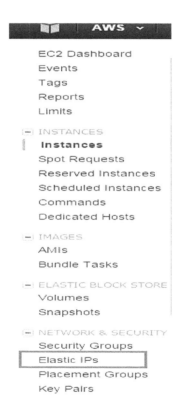

Step 2) Allocate a new Elastic IP Address.

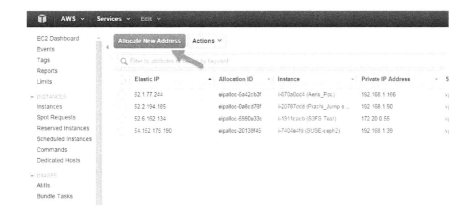

Step 3) Allocate this IP to be used in a VPC scope.

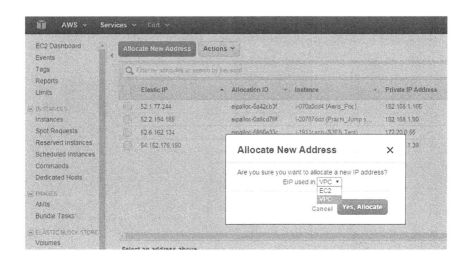

Your request will succeed if you don't have 5 or more than 5 EIPs already in your account.

Step 4) Now assign this IP to your instance.

1. Select the said IP

2. Click on Actions -> Associate Address

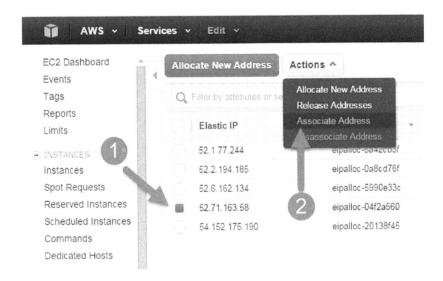

Step 5) In the next page,

1. Search for your instance and

2. Associate the IP to it.

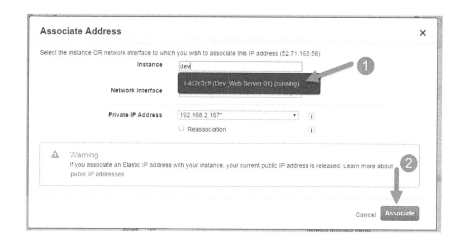

Step 6) Come back to your instances screen, you'll see that your instance has received your EIP.

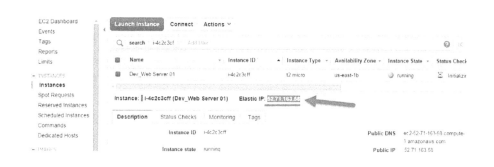

Step 7) Now open putty from your programs list and add your same EIP in there as below.

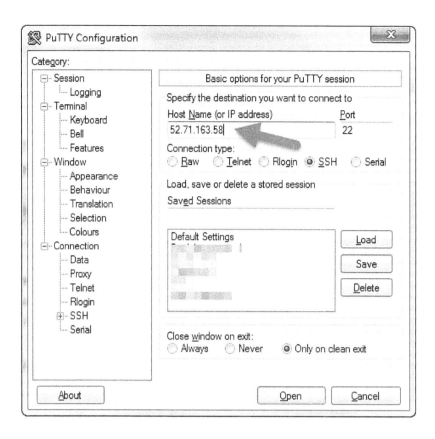

Step 8) In this step,

Add your private key in putty for secure connection

Go to Auth and Add your private key in .ppk (putty private key) format. You will need to convert pem file from AWS to ppk using puttygen. Once done click on "Open" button.

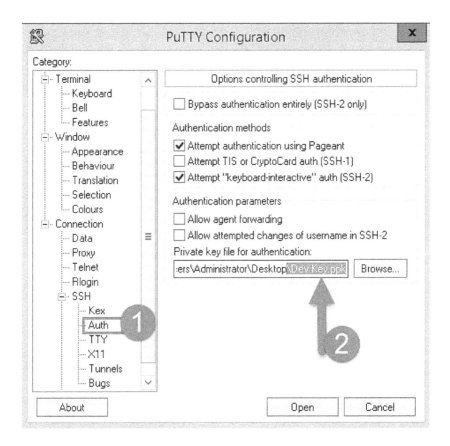

Once you connect, you will successfully see the Linux prompt.

Please note that the machine you are connecting from should be enabled on the instance Security Group for SSH (like in the steps above).

Once you become familiar with the above steps for launching the instance, it becomes a matter of 2 minutes to launch the same!

You can now use your on-demand EC2 server for your applications.

WHAT IS SPOT INSTANCE?

A spot Instance is an offering from AWS; it allows an AWS business subscriber to bid on unused AWS compute capacity. The hourly price for a Spot instance is decided by AWS, and it fluctuates depending on the supply and demand for Spot instances.

Your Spot instance runs whenever your bid exceeds the current market price. The price of a spot instance varies based on the instance type and the Availability Zone in which the instance can be provisioned.

When your bid price exceeds the market spot price of the instance called as the 'spot price,' your instance stays running. When the spot price overshoots the bid price, AWS will terminate your instance automatically. Therefore, it is necessary to plan the spot instances in your application architecture carefully.

CREATE A SPOT REQUEST

In order to launch a spot instance, you have to first create a Spot Request.

Follow the steps below to create a Spot Request.

1. On the EC2 Dashboard select 'Spot Requests' from the left pane under Instances.

2. Click on the button 'Request Spot Instances" as shown below.

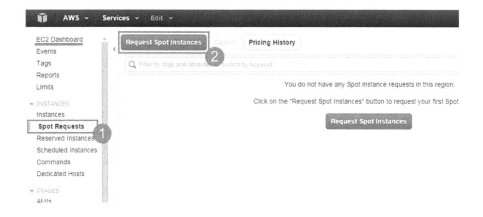

Spot instance launch wizard will open up. You can now go ahead with selecting the parameters and the instance configuration.

FIND INSTANCE TYPES

The first step for spot instance is to "Find instance types."

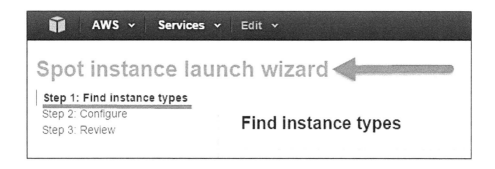

Step 1) Select an AMI- an AMI is a template consisting of the OS platform and software to be installed in the instance. Select your desired AMI from the existing list. We are selecting Amazon Linux AMI for this tutorial.

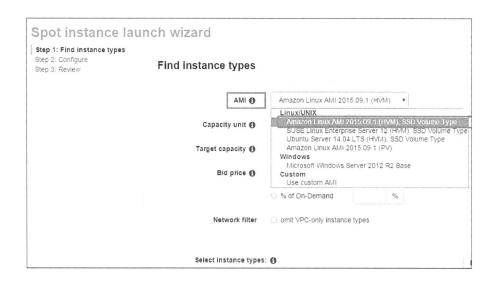

Step 2) Capacity Unit- a Capacity Unit is your application requirement. You may decide to launch an instance based on the instance type, vCPU or custom configuration like your choice of vCPU/memory/storage requirements. Here we are selecting an Instance.

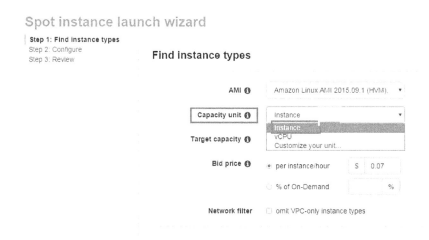

If you wish to customize the capacity, you can add your choice of

1. vCPU,

2. Memory and

3. Instance storage as below.

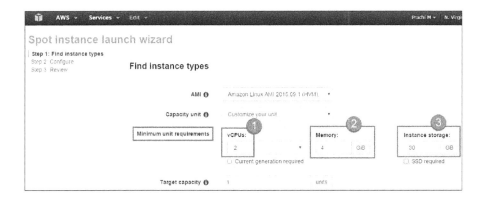

Step 3) Target Capacity depicts how many spot instances you wish to maintain in your request. Here we are selecting one.

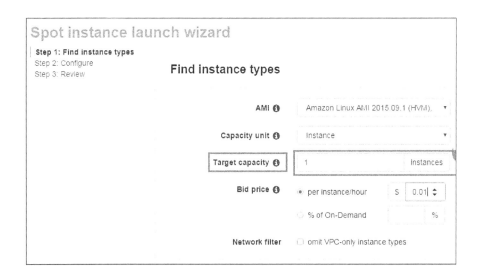

Step 4) Bid Price – this is the maximum price we are ready to pay for the instance. We are going to set a particular price per instance/hour. This is the simplest to calculate based on our business requirement. We will see ahead how we should determine the bid price so that our bid price always remains high and doesn't exceed the spot price so that our instance keeps running.

Spot instance launch wizard

Step 1: Find instance types
Step 2: Configure
Step 3: Review

Find instance types

AMI 🛈	Amazon Linux AMI 2015.09.1 (HVM). ▼
Capacity unit 🛈	Instance ▼
Target capacity 🛈	1 instances
Bid price 🛈	◉ per instance/hour $ 0.01 ↕
	○ % of On-Demand %
Network filter	☐ omit VPC-only instance types

just below the bid price you can see a button of Pricing History. Click on that as shown below.

Bid price 🛈	◉ per instance/hour	$ 0.07
	○ % of On-Demand	%
Network filter	☐ omit VPC-only instance types	

Select instance types: 🛈   Pricing History   Spot Bid Advisor

Instance type ▼	vCPUs ▼	Memory (GiB) ▼	Storage (GB) ▼	Weighted capacity 🛈	Total bid price 🛈 ▼	% of On-Demand ▼
All instance types ▼	1 ▼	(Any)	(Any)	✎	✎	
☐ c3.large	2	3.75	2 x 16 SSD	1	$0.07	67%

Here in Pricing History, we can see a graph depicting instance pricing trends with historical data. You can select the parameters and get an idea of the pricing of our desired instance over a period of time.

1. Select the product. We have selected our Linux AMI.

2. Select the instance type. We have selected m3.medium.

3. Note the average prices for over a day here.

Thus, from the chart below, we can see that the instance type that we are planning to provision lies in the pricing range of $0.01xx, and it seems that Availability Zone 'us-east 1a' has the lowest price.

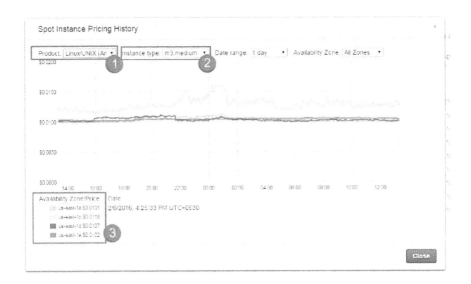

cont. to step 4.

So let's come back to our step of quoting a bid price.

For the sake of maintaining our instance always available and if it falls within our budget, we can quote a higher bid price. Here we have quoted a slightly higher price of $0.05.

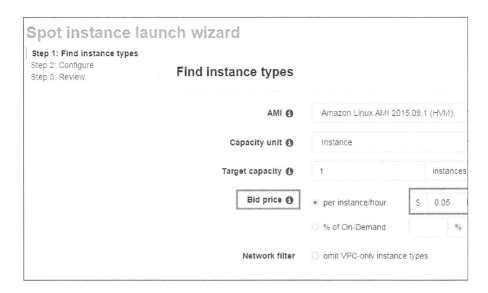

You can see some trends in the wizard itself.

1. Note the instance types section

2. Select the instance type that we are planning to provision

3. Note the price that we are planning to bid. % of on-demand shows us that our quoted price is 75% of the on-demand price for the same instance type. This means we are saving 25% per hour as compared to an on-demand instance. You can further lower the price and save costs drastically.

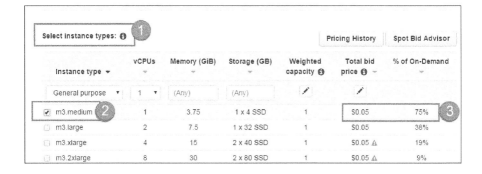

Step 5) Once we are done looking at the trends and quoting our bid price, click on next.

Select instance types: ⓘ					Pricing History		Spot Bid Advisor
Instance type ▼	vCPUs ▼	Memory (GiB) ▼	Storage (GB) ▼	Weighted capacity ⓘ	Total bid price ⓘ ▼	% of On-Demand ▼
General purpose ▼	1 ▼	(Any)	(Any)	✏	✏	
☑ m3.medium	1	3.75	1 x 4 SSD	1	$0.05	75%
☐ m3.large	2	7.5	1 x 32 SSD	1	$0.05	38%
☐ m3.xlarge	4	15	2 x 40 SSD	1	$0.05 ⚠	19%
☐ m3.2xlarge	8	30	2 x 80 SSD	1	$0.05 ⚠	9%
☐ m4.large	2	8	EBS only	1	$0.05	42%
☐ m4.xlarge	4	16	EBS only	1	$0.05	21%
☐ m4.2xlarge	8	32	EBS only	1	$0.05 ⚠	10%
☐ m4.4xlarge	16	64	EBS only	1	$0.05 ⚠	5%
☐ m4.10xlarge	40	160	EBS only	1	$0.05 ⚠	2%
			view more			

Cancel   Next

CONFIGURE THE SPOT INSTANCE

Our next step is to configure the instance, in this step of the wizard, we'll configure instance parameters like VPC, subnets, etc.

Let's take a look.

Step 1) Allocation Strategy – it determines how your spot request is fulfilled from the AWS's spot pools. There are two types of strategies:

- Diversified – here, spot instances are balanced across all the spot pools

- Lowest price – here, spot instances are launched from the pool which has lowest price offers

For this tutorial, we'll select Lowest Price as our allocation strategy.

Step 2) Select the VPC- we'll select from the list of available VPCs that we have created earlier. We can also create a new VPC in this step.

Step 3) Next we'll select the security group for the instance. We can select an already existing SG or create a new one.

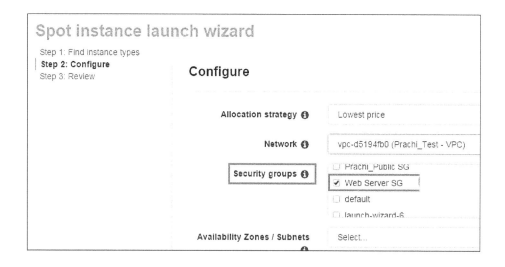

Step 4) Availability Zone- we'll select the AZ where we want to place our instance based on our application architecture. We are selecting AZ- us-east-1a.

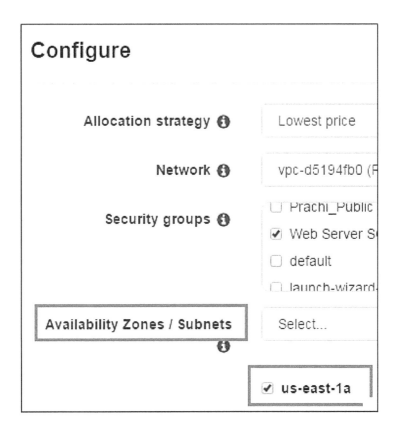

Step 5) Subnets- we are going to select the subnet from our list of already available list.

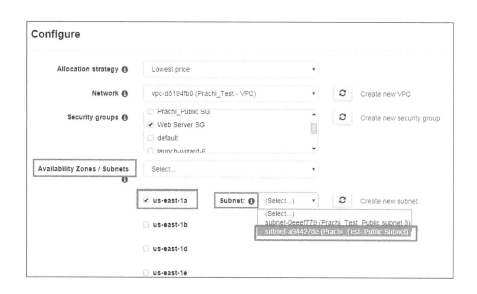

Step 6) Public IP- we'll choose to assign the instance a public IP as soon as it launches. In this step, you can choose if you want AWS to assign it an IP automatically, or you want to do it manually later. You can enable/ disable 'Auto assign Public IP' feature here likewise.

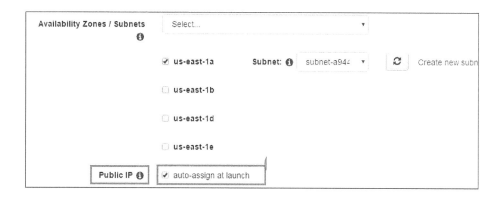

Step 7) Key pair- A key pair is a set of public-private keys.

AWS stores the private key in the instance, and you are asked to download the public key. Make sure you download the key and keep it safe and secured; if it is lost you cannot download it again.

After selecting public IP, here we are selecting a key which we already have created in our last tutorial.

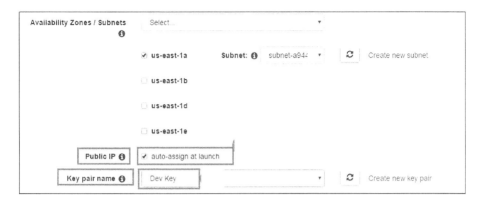

REVIEW YOUR SPOT INSTANCE

Once we are done configuring our spot instance request in the 2 steps earlier in our wizard, we'll take a look at the overall configuration.

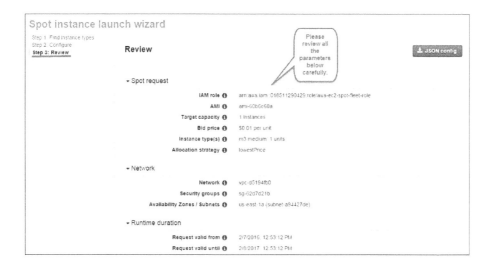

We can also download a JSON file with all the configurations. Below is our JSON file

After we are done reviewing, we can proceed with the launching by clicking the Launch button as shown below.

Once we select Launch, we can see a notification about the request getting created.

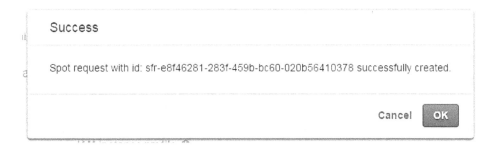

The spot request creation wizard will close, and the page will automatically direct back to the EC2 Dashboard.

You can see as shown below that the State of our request is 'open' which means that it is getting evaluated from the AWS's side. AWS EC2 will check if the required instance is available in its spot pool.

After a couple of minutes, you can see that the state is changed to 'active', and now our spot request is successfully fulfilled. You can note the configuration parameters below.

SUMMARY

Thus, we saw in detail how to create an on-demand EC2 instance in this tutorial. Because it is an on-demand server, you can keep it running when in use and 'Stop' it when it's unused to save on your costs.

You can provision a Linux or Windows EC2 instance or from any of the available AMIs in AWS Marketplace based on your choice of OS platform.

If your application is in production and you have to use it for years to come, you should consider provisioning a reserved instance to drastically save on your CAPEX.

Here, we saw how to create a Spot Instance request successfully by determining our bid price.

Spot instances are a great way to save on costs for instances which are not application critical. A common example would be to create a fleet of spot instances for a task such as image processing or video encoding. In such cases, you can keep a cluster of instances under a load balancer.

If the bid price exceeds the spot price and your instance is terminated from AWS's side, you can have other instances doing the processing job for you. You can leverage Auto scaling for this scenario. Avoid using Spot instances for business critical applications like databases etc.

CHANGE INSTANCE TYPE, SECURITY GROUP, TERMINATION PROTECTION: AWS EC2

EC2 stands for Elastic Compute Cloud. It is the compute service offering from the IaaS (Infrastructure as a Service) area of AWS.

Once an EC2 instance is provisioned, it is very handy to update/modify many of the instances configuration parameters using AWS Management Console.

Let's take a look at each of them.

What You Will Learn:

- Login and access to AWS services
- Checke the modification parameters
- View the connection details
- Launch multiple instances with the similar configuration
- Change the instance state
- Change instance settings
- Create tags
- Attach to Auto Scaling Group
- Change instance type
- Enable termination protection
- Change User Data
- Change the shutdown behavior
- View System Log

- Create an instance AMI
- Change the instance network settings
- Change the Security Group
- Add a Network Interface
- Dissociating EIP
- Change Source/Destination check
- Manag private IP addresses
- Enable/disable ClassicLink to a VPC
- Enable detailed CloudWatch monitoring

LOGIN AND ACCESS TO AWS SERVICES

Step 1) In this step, you will do

Login to your AWS account and go to the AWS Services tab at the top left corner.

Here, you will see all of the AWS Services categorized as per their area viz. Compute, Storage, Database, etc. For creating an EC2 instance, we have to choose Compute EC2 as in the next step.

Open all the services and click on EC2 under Compute services. This will launch the dashboard of EC2.

Here is the EC2 dashboard. Here you will get all the information in gist about the AWS EC2 resources running.

Step 2) On the top right corner of the EC2 dashboard, choose the AWS Region in which you want to provision the EC2 server.

Here we are selecting N. Virginia. AWS provides 10 Regions all over the globe.

Step 3) Once your desired Region is selected, come back to the EC2 Dashboard.

CHECKE THE MODIFICATION PARAMETERS

Step 1) On the EC2 Dashboard, select the instance whose configuration parameters you want to modify and Click on the "Actions" button as shown below.

Step 2) As you click the button, the drop- down will show us all the areas where we can modify the instance characteristics.

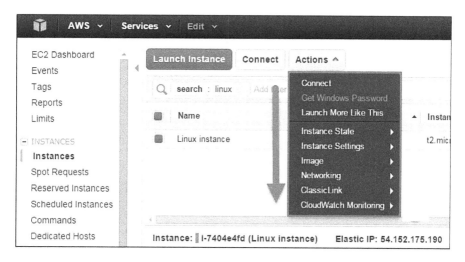

VIEW THE CONNECTION DETAILS

Connect option below will show us ways in which we can connect to an EC2 instance.

Step 1) Click on option 'Connect.'

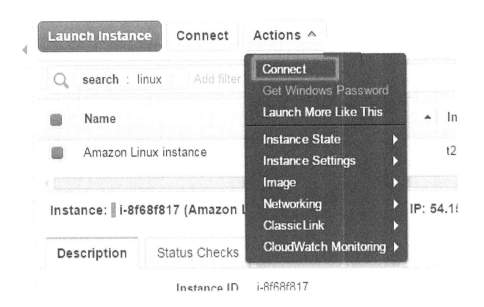

You may choose to connect with a standalone SSH client or a Java client. You will get a step-by-step procedure on how you can connect to your instance.

For this tutorial, we can see the connection methods for a Linux instance.

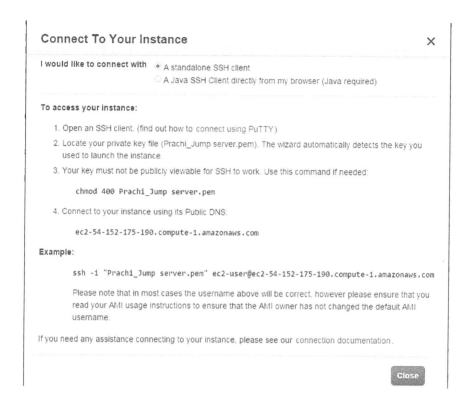

LAUNCH MULTIPLE INSTANCES WITH THE SIMILAR CONFIGURATION

If you have a single EC2 instance running with a particular configuration, and you wish to quickly launch another instance in a one-click deployment, then 'Launch More Like This' option helps us do that.

Step 1) Click on 'Launch More Like This.'

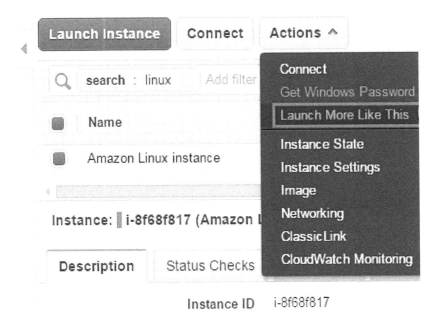

You will be straightaway directed to the review instance details page of the launch instance wizard. Here we can verify all the details once more.

Step 2) On review instance details page Click on button 'Launch.'

Step 3) In this window,

1. Select an existing key pair

2. Click on "Launch Instance."

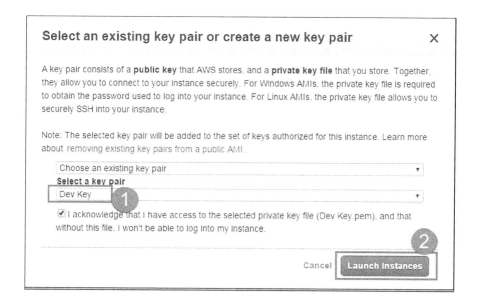

Instance launch progress can be seen as below.

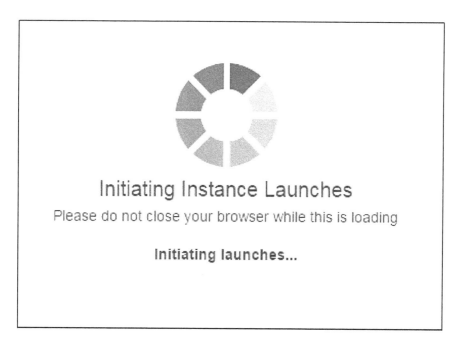

You can see below that a new instance is in a pending state before creation.

You can see that the new instance has the same tag as well.

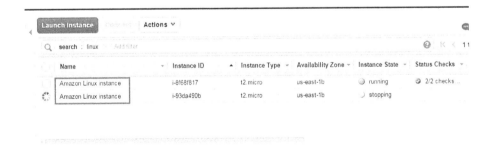

CHANGE THE INSTANCE STATE

You can change the instance state on the fly from the Management Console on a single click.

Step 1) In this step, Click on 'Instance State' under actions.

- Stop – you can stop the running instance

- Reboot – you can reboot the instance

- Terminate – you can delete the instance permanently

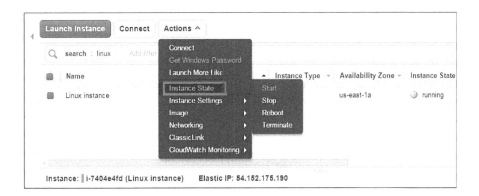

CHANGE INSTANCE SETTINGS

Here you can change a lot of instance settings like security groups, termination protection, etc.

Let's us see each one in detail.

CREATE TAGS

Add/Edit Tags – You can add or edit the tags assigned to the instance. Tagging makes it easier for the business owner of the AWS account to keep a track of the instances especially if there are multiple environments.

AWS admins should assign each instance a tag based on the segregation e.g.: tagging all the instances in the production environment as 'Prod' or tagging the instances belonging to a department with the department initials etc. Tagging is a very effective method to track the costing of the instances as well.

Let's see how to change tags

Step 1) In this step,

1. Click on instance setting

2. Click on 'Add/Edit Tags.'

Step 2) A tag is just a key-value pair.

1. So we have assigned a new tag as Department and added its value as Cloud.

2. Click on Save

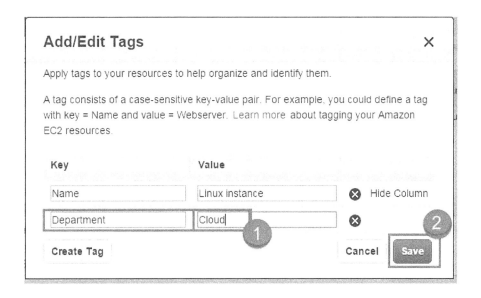

Step 3) Come back to the EC2 Dashboard and

1. Select your instance again

2. Select the tab of 'Tags'

Note that the new tag as "Department" with value as Cloud has appeared under Tags.

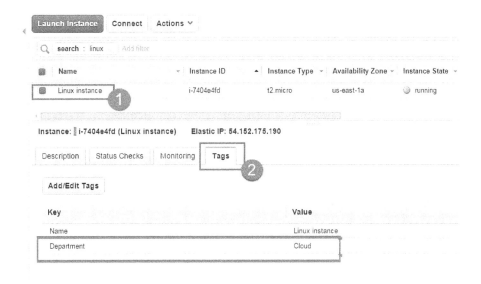

ATTACH TO AUTO SCALING GROUP

An EC2 instance can be attached to an Auto Scaling Group on the fly.

Step 1) In this step, we do following things

1. Click on 'Instance Settings'

2. Click on 'Attach to Auto Scaling Group.'

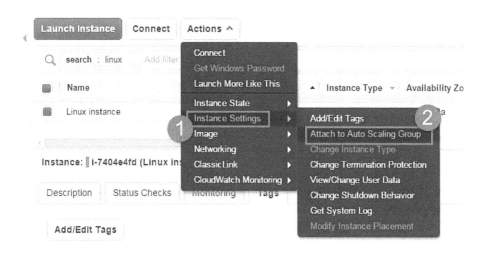

Step 2) In this step,

1. Attach an instance to an existing AS group. You can also create a new AS group in this step.

2. Select one AS group from the list of already existing groups.

3. Click on 'Attach'.

This action will attach your instance to an auto-scaling group in your environment.

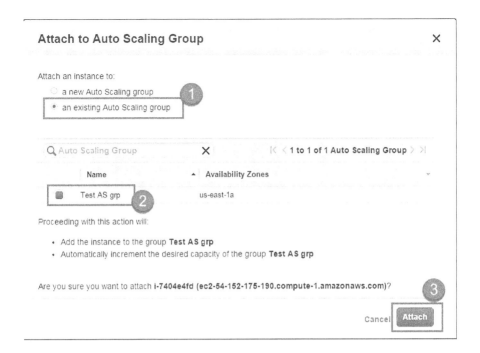

CHANGE INSTANCE TYPE

You can change the instance-type of your instance if you desire higher configuration instance as per your application requirement. This can be done to vertically scale your instance and provide you with more compute/memory capacity.

Let's see how to do this.

You cannot change an instance type if it's a running server. You have to stop it before doing so.

Step 1) In this step,

1. Go to 'Instance State'

2. Click on 'Stop'. This will stop the instance.

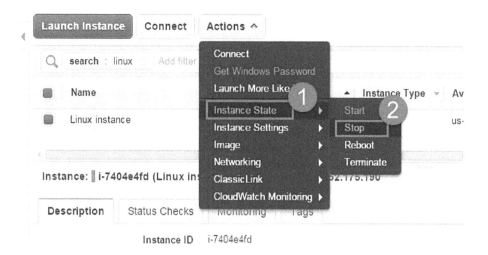

Note that the instance state is now in "stopping" mode on the EC2 Dashboard. You change an instance type now.

Step 2) In this step,

1. Go to 'Instance Settings'

2. Click on 'Change Instance Type'

A Change Instance Type pop-up will appear.

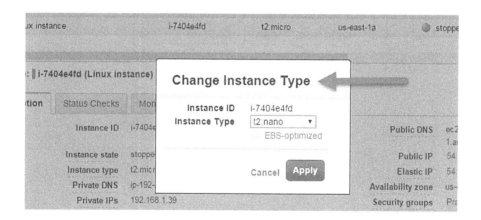

Step 3) You can select from a range of EC2 available instance types. For this tutorial, we are changing it to t2.nano just for the sake of demonstration.

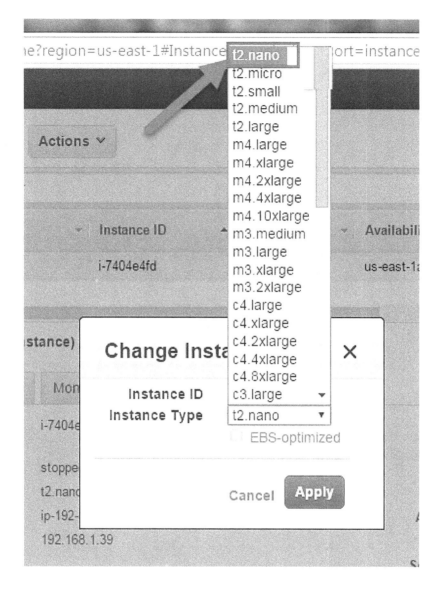

Step 4) Select t2.nano and hit 'Apply'.

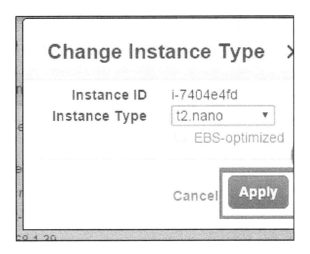

Notice on the EC2 Dashboard, your instance type has been changed to the said type automatically.

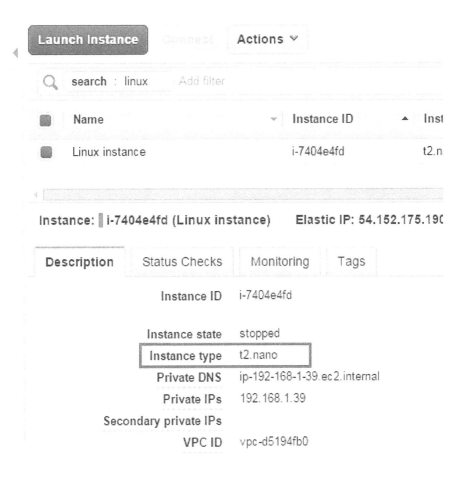

You can now start your instance and continue on the operations on that. There will be no change in other configuration parameters and also your existing installations on the server will remain intact.

ENABLE TERMINATION PROTECTION

An instance should always have termination protection enabled especially on production servers. This will ensure that your EC2 instance is not getting accidently terminated.

AWS will add an additional level of security in case you happen to accidently hit the instance terminate option.

Let's see how to enable termination protection.

Step 1) In this step,

1. Go to 'Instance Settings.'

2. Click on 'Change Termination Protection.'

Step 2) Notice that the current setting on our instance is disabled. Click on "Yes, Enable".

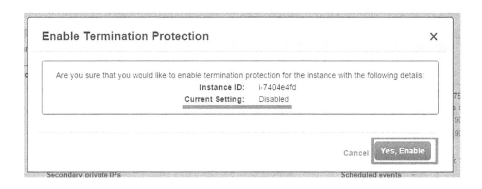

This has enabled Termination protection on our instance. We'll check to see if our instance gets deleted when we hit Terminate.

Step 3) In this step,

1. Select option 'Instance State' and then

2. Click on 'Terminate.'

m

AWS will immediately notify you that the EC2 instance has "termination protection enabled" and you will not be able to delete it. The 'Terminate' button below is disabled.

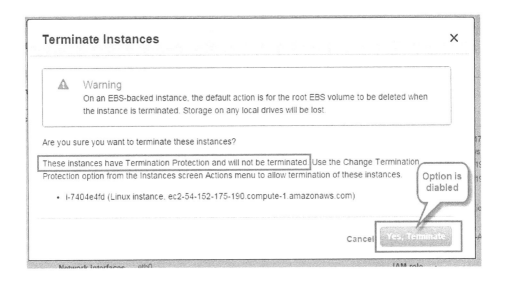

CHANGE USER DATA

When you launch a new EC2 instance, you have the option to pass user data to an instance to run tasks at boot time automatically e.g. common configuration tasks, init scripts, etc.

You can pass the user data in the form of shell scripts or cloud-init directives. This can be either plain text, as a file or as base64 encoded text for API calls.

Here we will see how we can edit these scripts.

You will have to stop the instance first, you will not be able to edit the instance userdata if it's running. On a stopped instance, perform below steps.

Step 1) In this step, do the following things

1. Go to 'Instance Settings'.

2. Click on 'View/Change User Data'.

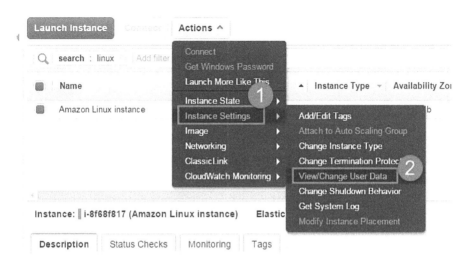

Here for the purpose of demonstration, we have a shell script which installs LAMP stack on the server.

Step 2) In this step,

1. View/ modify your user data field.

2. Click on "Save" tab.

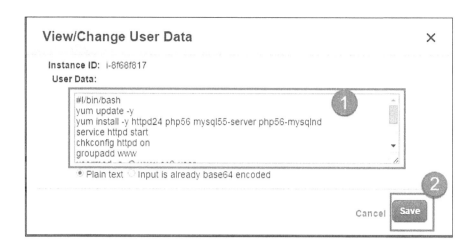

CHANGE THE SHUTDOWN BEHAVIOR

If ever you have accidently shutdown the instance via the OS console, you don't want AWS EC2 to actually terminate the instance.

For that, we can set up the shutdown behavior as 'Stop' instead of 'Terminate'. We can also do vice versa if the application requirement is as such.

Let's see how to achieve this.

Step 1) In this step,

1. Go to 'Instance Settings'.

2. Click on 'Change Shutdown Behavior.'

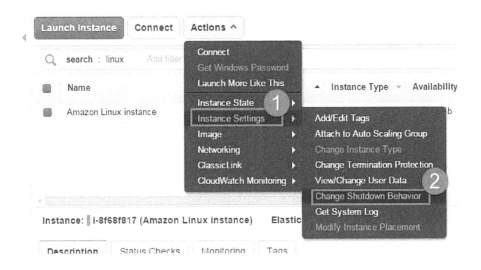

Step 2) In this step, click on 'Stop' and then hit apply. The setting will be applied to the instance accordingly.

Step 3) Now when "stop" shutdown is initiated in the instance console via putty, it will not get terminated. It will simply shutdown normally.

```
ec2-user@ip-192-168-2-119:~

[ec2-user@ip-192-168-2-119 ~]$ shutdown now
shutdown: Need to be root
[ec2-user@ip-192-168-2-119 ~]$ sudo shutdown now

Broadcast message from ec2-user@ip-192-168-2-119
        (/dev/pts/0) at 10:12 ...

The system is going down for maintenance NOW!
[ec2-user@ip-192-168-2-119 ~]$ █
```

VIEW SYSTEM LOG

You can see the system log for any EC2 instance for troubleshooting purposes etc.

Step 1) In this step,

1. Go to 'Instance Settings'.

2. Click on 'Get System Log'.

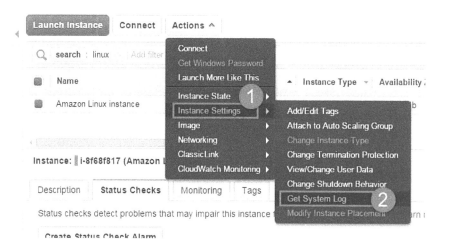

You can see a separate window depicting the instance log details. Here we can see a snap of log when the instance was restarted.

```
System Log: i-8f68f817 (Amazon Linux instance)                          ↻ ×

Stopping auditd: [  338.460244] audit: type=1305 audit(1455099123.120:35): audit_pid=0 old
[  OK  ]
[  338.558605] audit: type=1305 audit(1455099123.212:36): auid=4294967295 ses=4294967295 o
[  338.565151] audit: type=1305 audit(1455099123.220:37): audit_enabled=0 old=1 auid=42949
Shutting down system logger: [  OK  ]
Shutting down interface eth0: [  OK  ]
Shutting down loopback interface: [  OK  ]
Stopping rngd: [  OK  ]
Retrigger failed udev events--type=failed is deprecated and will be removed from a future
udevadm[2629]: --type=failed is deprecated and will be removed from a future udev release.

[  OK  ]
[H[JTelling INIT to go to single user mode.
init: rc main process (2386) killed by TERM signal
/dev/fd/10: line 2: plymouth: command not found
[root@ip-192-168-2-119 /]# /dev/fd/9: line 1: /sbin/plymouthd: No such file or directory
init: plymouth-shutdown main process (2665) terminated with status 1
initctl: Event failed
init: splash-manager main process (2661) terminated with status 1
Stopping block device availability: Deactivating block devices:
[  OK  ]
Sending all processes the TERM signal... [  OK  ]
Sending all processes the KILL signal... init: rcS-sulogin main process (2638) killed by K
[  OK  ]
Saving random seed: [  OK  ]
Turning off quotas: [  OK  ]
init: Re-executing /sbin/init
[ 1402.297137] EXT4-fs (xvda1): re-mounted. Opts: (null)
Please stand by while rebooting the system...
[ 1402.456859] xenbus: xenbus_dev_shutdown: device/vfb/0: Initialising != Connected, skipp
[ 1402.462662] reboot: Restarting system
[ 1402.465001] reboot: machine restart
◄                                                                        ►

                                                                    Close
```

CREATE AN INSTANCE AMI

You can create an AMI of your EC2 instance for backup.

Step 1) In this step,

1. Go to 'Image'.

2. Click on 'Create Image'.

An image creation wizard will open.

Step 2) In this step,

1. Add the image name

2. Give some friendly description for the AMI

3. Check the volumes and then hit 'Create Image' button.

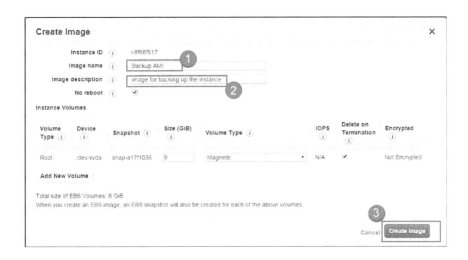

AWS will receive your create image request and will send a notification immediately.

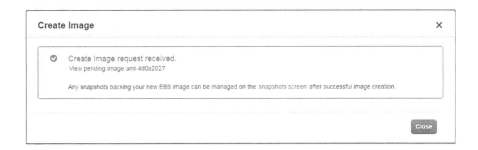

You can check the status of the request on the EC2 dashboard as 'pending' just like what is shown below.

After a while the status is "available" and you will have your AMI ready as a backup.

You can also de-register it from the dashboard once the backup is old.

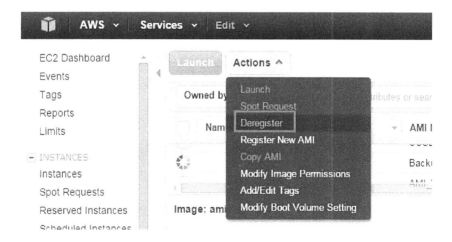

CHANGE THE INSTANCE NETWORK SETTINGS

CHANGE THE SECURITY GROUP

You can change the SG (Security Group) of an instance anytime. If you have another security group with different firewall rules, you can easily do so using the console.

Let's see how.

Step 1) In this step,

1. Go to 'Networking'.

2. Click on 'Change Security Groups'.

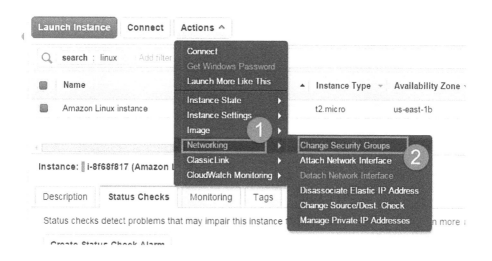

Step 2) In the change security groups wizard, it will show the already existing SG on the instance along with a list of all the security groups in the region.

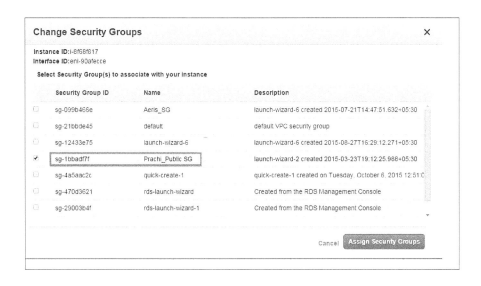

Step 3) In this step,

1. Tick the box against your desired SG

2. Click on 'Assign Security Groups' button.

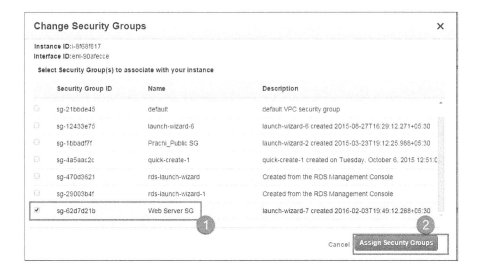

Step 4) On the EC2 Dashboard, you can see that the SG of the instance has been changed. The instance will now send/receive traffic based on the new SG settings.

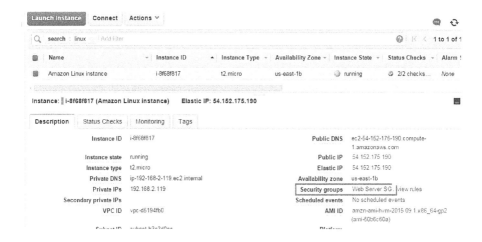

You can also add multiple security groups.

ADD A NETWORK INTERFACE

A network interface is like another NIC card to an instance. It will have another set of IPs additional to the already existing primary Network Interface.

Step 1) In this step,

1. Go to 'Networking'.

2. Click on 'Attach Network Interface'.

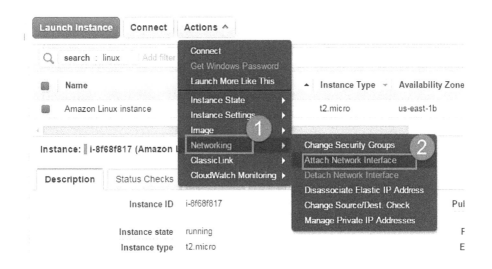

You will get an error prompt if you don't have a Network Interface already created.

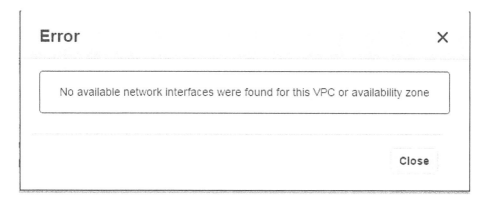

Let's see how to create a Network Interface quickly.

Step 2) In this step,

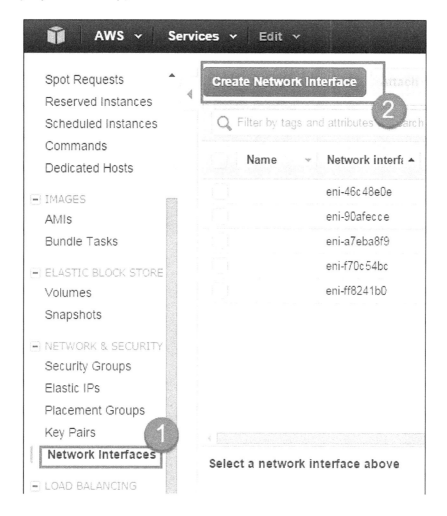

1. Go to EC2 Dashboard, and click on 'Network Interfaces' on the left pane.

2. Click on 'Create Network Interface' button.

Step 3) In this step,

1. Add a description for your network interface

2. Select the subnet where you want to create your network interface. Keep the auto assign the private IP option default

3. Security groups are applied to a network interface of an instance, so here you will get an option for the same. Select your desired SG

4. Once you're done entering the details, click on 'Create.'

Now you can come back to the EC2 Dashboard and check that your network interface is getting created.

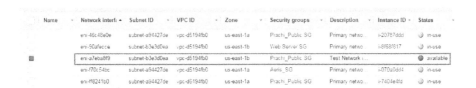

Now come back on Step 2) and go ahead with selecting your available interface which we just created and attach it to the instance.

Now as you can see the network interface which we just created is enlisted below automatically.

Your network interface will be attached to the instance immediately.

We can come back to the EC2 Dashboard and check our instance now. Note that the instance has 2 private IPs belonging to 2 network interfaces.

DISSOCIATING EIP

An Elastic IP is a static Public IP.

You can dissociate an EIP directly from the instance dashboard.

Step 1) In this step,

1. Click on 'Networking.'

2. Click on 'Dissociate Elastic IP Address.'

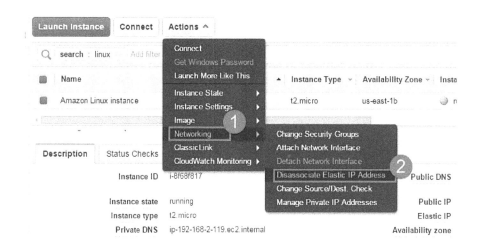

Step 2) Click on the button of dissociate, once we have verified the instance id and the EIP.

Check below that the instance dashboard now shows the EIP field blank.

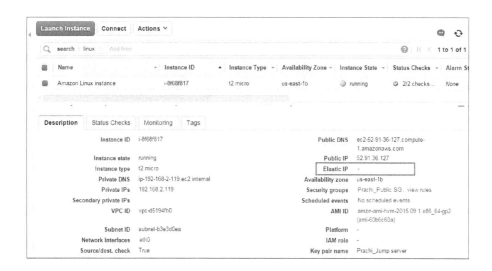

CHANGE SOURCE/DESTINATION CHECK

The Source/Destination Check attribute controls whether source/destination checking is enabled on the instance. Disabling this attribute enables an instance to handle network traffic that isn't specifically destined for the instance. For example, instances running services such as network address translation, routing, or a firewall should set this value to disabled.

Step 1) In this step,

1. Click on 'Networking.'

2. Click on 'change Source/Dust. Check'

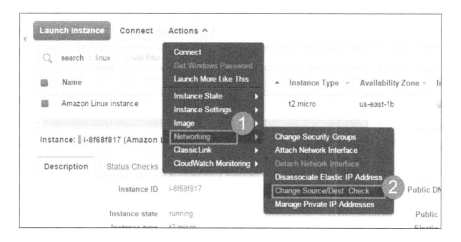

Step 2) Click on 'Disable'. If it is disabled already, you can enable it in this step.

MANAGE PRIVATE IP ADDRESSES

You can assign multiple private IP addresses to a single instance if that is your application architecture's design. The maximum no of IPs you can assign of course depends on the EC2 instance type.

Step 1) In this step

1. Click on 'Networking.'

2. Click on 'Manage Private IP addresses.'

You will be redirected to a new window to assign a secondary IP address to your instance.

Step 2) In this step,

1. Here we are leaving the field blank. This will enable AWS to auto-assign any available private IP to our instance.

2. Click on 'Update.'

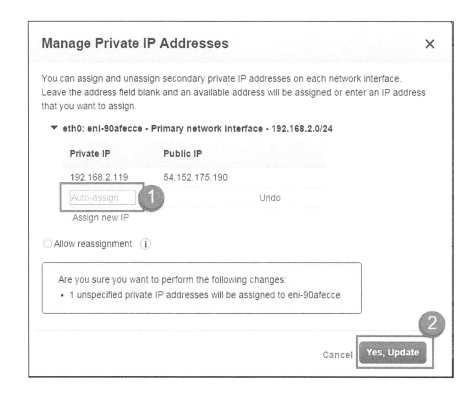

Note that an IP has been automatically assigned here.

Also, come back to the EC2 dashboard and notice the 2 private IPs assigned. These are 2 IPs on a single network interface.

ENABLE/DISABLE CLASSICLINK TO A VPC

If your instance is provisioned in EC2 – Classic, which is a deployment mode in AWS where resources are provisioned out of a VPC; then you can link your instance to a VPC environment as shown below.

The options below are disabled for us as our instance is already in a VPC.

ENABLE DETAILED CLOUDWATCH MONITORING

AWS will by default have basic CloudWatch monitoring enabled on all its resources. However, if our instances are production instances, we may wish to enable detailed monitoring on them with additional costs of course.

Step 1) In this step,

1. Click on 'CloudWatch Monitoring'

2. Click on 'Enable Detailed Monitoring'

You can also add/edit alarms to alert you for attributes in your CloudWatch monitoring metrics.

SUMMARY

Thus, we saw in this tutorial, how to enable/modify various attributes in AWS for the instance configuration from the Management Console after it is launched.

AWS provides many more configuration options via CLI/API.

WHAT IS AWS LAMBDA? LAMBDA FUNCTION WITH EXAMPLES

Before AWS Lambda, let's understand:

What is Serverless?

Serverless is a term that generally refers to serverless applications. Serverless applications are ones that don't need any server provision and do not require to manage servers.

What is AWS Lambda?

AWS Lambda is one such serverless compute service. Therefore you don't need to worry about which AWS resources to launch, or how will they manage them. Instead, you need to put the code on Lambda, and it runs. However, a lambda can only be used to execute background tasks.

In AWS Lambda the code is executed based on the response of events in AWS services such as add/delete files in S3 bucket, HTTP request from Amazon API gateway, etc.

AWS Lambda also helps you to focus on your core product and business logic instead of manages operating system (OS) access control, OS patching, right-sizing, provisioning, scaling, etc.

In this AWS Lambda tutorial for beginners, you will learn:

- What is Serverless?
- What is AWS Lambda?
- How does AWS Lambda work?
- Events that Trigger AWS Lambda
- AWS Lambda Concepts
- AWS Lambda VS AWS EC2
- AWS Lambda VS AWS Elastic Beanstalk
- Use Cases of AWS Lambda
- Best practices of Lambda function
- When not to use AWS Lambda
- Advantages of using AWS Lambda
- Limitations of AWS Lambda

HOW DOES AWS LAMBDA WORK?

The following block diagram explains the working of AWS Lambda in a few easy steps:

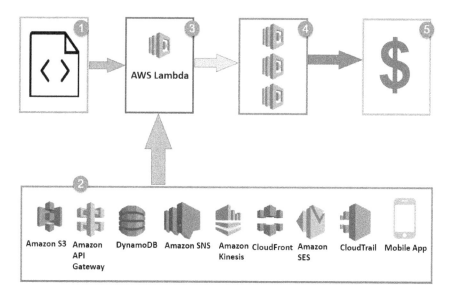

Step 1: First upload your AWS Lambda code in any language supported by AWS Lambda. Java, Python, Go, and C# are some of the languages that are supported by AWS lambda.

Step 2: These are some AWS services which allow you to trigger AWS Lambda.

Step 3: AWS Lambda helps you to upload code and the event details on which it should be triggered.

Step 4: Executes AWS Lambda Code when it is triggered by AWS services:

Step 5: AWS charges only when the AWS lambda code executes, and not otherwise.

This will happen in the following scenarios:

- Upload files in an S3 bucket
- When HTTP get/post endpoint URL is hit
- For adding/modifying and deleting Dynamo DB tables
- In the process of data streams collection
- Push notification
- Hosting of website
- Email sending

Note: You should remember that you will charge for AWS services only when the AWS Lambda code executes, else you don't need to pay anything.

EVENTS THAT TRIGGER AWS LAMBDA

Here, are Events which will be triggered when you use AWS Lambda.

- Insert, updating and deleting data Dynamo DB table
- To include push notifications in SNS
- To search for log history in CloudTrail
- Entry into an S3 object
- DynamoDB can trigger AWS Lambda whenever there is data added, modified, and deleted in the table.
- Helps you to schedule the event to carry out the task at regular time pattern.
- Modifications to objects in S3 buckets
- Notifications sent from Amazon SNS.
- AWS Lambda can be used to process the CloudTrail logs
- API Gateway allows you to trigger AWS Lambda on GET/POST methods.

AWS LAMBDA CONCEPTS

Function:

A function is a program or a script which runs in AWS Lambda. Lambda passes invocation events into your function, which processes an event and returns its response.

Runtimes:

Runtime allows functions in various languages which runs on the same base execution environment. This helps you to configure your function in runtime. It also matches your selected programming language.

Event source:

An event source is an AWS service, such as Amazon SNS, or a custom service. This triggers function helps you to executes its logic.

Lambda Layers:

Lambda layers are an important distribution mechanism for libraries, custom runtimes, and other important function dependencies. This AWS component also helps you to manage your development function code separately from the unchanging code and resources that it uses.

Log streams:

Log stream allows you to annotate your function code with custom logging statements which helps you to analyse the execution flow and performance of your Lambda functions.

HOW TO USE AWS LAMBDA

Step 1) Goto https://aws.amazon.com/lambda/ and Get Started

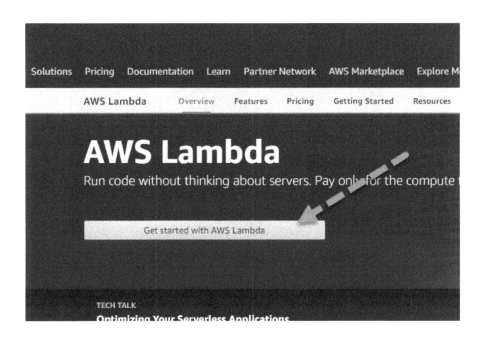

Step 2) Create an account or sign in with your existing account

Step 3) In the next Lambda page,

Edit the code and Click Run.

Step 4) You will see output

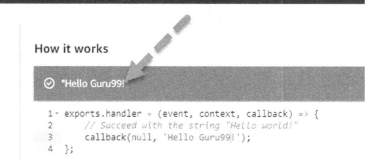

AWS LAMBDA VS AWS EC2

Here, are some major differences between AWS Lambda and EC2.

Parameters	AWS Lambda	AWS EC2
Definition	AWS Lambda is a Platform as a Service (PaaS). It helps you to run and execute your backend code.	AWS EC2 Is an Infrastructure as a Service (IaaS). It provides virtualized computing resources.

Flexibility	Does not offers any flexibility to log in to compute instances. It allows you to choose a customized operating system or language runtime.	Offers the flexibility to select the variety of instances, customoperating systems, security patches, and network, etc.
Installation process	You need to select your environment where you want to runthe code and push the code into AWS Lambda.	For the first time in EC2, you have to choose the OS and install all the software required and then push your code in EC2.
Environment restrictions	It is restricted to fewlanguages.	No environment restrictions.

AWS LAMBDA VS AWS ELASTIC BEANSTALK

Here, are some major differences between AWS Lambda and Elastic Beanstalk.

Parameters	AWS Elastic Beanstalk	AWS Lambda
Main task	Deploy and manage the apps on AWS Cloud without worrying about the infrastructure which runs those applications.	AWS Lambda is used for running and executing your Back-end code. You can't use it to deploy an application.

Selection of AWS resources	It gives you a Freedom to select AWS resources; For example, you can choose EC2 instance which is optimal according to your application.	You can't select the AWS resources, like a type of EC2 instance, Lambda offers resources based on your workload.
Type of system	It is a stateful system.	It is a stateless system.

USE CASES OF AWS LAMBDA

AWS Lambda used for a wide range of applications like:

- Helps you for ETL process
- Allows you to perform real-time file processing and real-time stream processing
- Use for creating web applications
- Use in Amazon products like Alexa Chatbots and Amazon Echo/Alexa
- Data processing (real-time streaming analytics)
- Automated Backups of everyday tasks
- Scalable back ends (mobile apps, IoT devices)
- Helps you to execute server-side backend logic
- Allows you to filter and Transform data

BEST PRACTICES OF LAMBDA FUNCTION

Here, are important best practices of Lambda functions:

- Use the right "timeout."
- Utilize the functions of local storage which is 500MB in size in the /temp folder
- Minimizing the use of start-up code which is not directly related to processing the current event.
- You should use built-in CloudWatch monitoring of your Lambda functions to view and optimize request latencies.

WHEN NOT TO USE AWS LAMBDA

Following are the situation where Lambda is surely not an ideal option:

- It is not appropriate to use AWS Lambda software packages or applications which rely on calling underlying Windows RPCs
- If is used for custom software applications with licensing agreements like MS-Office document processing, Oracle databases, etc.
- AWS Lambda should not be used for custom hardware process such as GPU acceleration, hardware affinity.

ADVANTAGES OF USING AWS LAMBDA

Here, are pros/benefits of using AWS lambda:

- AWS Lambda is a highly flexible tool to use
- It helps you to grant access to resources, including VPCs

- Author directly with WYSIWYG editor in console.
- You can use it as a plugin for Eclipse and Visual Studio.
- As it is serverless architecture, you don't need to worry about managing or provisioning servers.
- You do not need to set up any Virtual Machine.
- Helps developers to run and execute the code's response to events without building any infrastructure.
- You just need to for the compute time taken, only when your code runs.
- You can monitor your code performance in real time through CloudWatch.
- It allows you to run your code without provisioning or to manage any other server
- Helps you to execute the code only when needed
- You can scale it automatically to handle a few requests per day and even support more than thousands of requests per second.
- AWS Lambda can be configured with the help of external event timers to perform scheduled tasks.
- AWS Lambda should be configured with external event and timers so; it can be used for scheduling.
- Lambda functions are stateless so that it can be scaled quickly.
- AWS Lambda is fast so it will execute your code within milliseconds.

LIMITATIONS OF AWS LAMBDA

Here are the cons/disadvantages of using AWS Lambda:

- AWS Lambda tool is not suitable for small projects.

- AWS Lambda entirely relies on AWS for the infrastructure, so you can't install any additional software if your code demands it.
- Concurrent execution is limited to 100
- AWS Lambda completely depended on AWS for the infrastructure; you cannot install anything additional software if your code demands it.
- Its memory volume can vary between 128 to 1536 MB.
- Event request should not exceed 128 KB.
- Lambda functions help you to write their logs only in CloudWatch. This is the only tool that allows you to monitor or troubleshoot your functions.
- Its code execution timeout is just 5 minutes.

SUMMARY

- Serverless is a term that generally refers to serverless applications.
- AWS Lambda is one such serverless compute service. Therefore, you don't need to worry about which AWS resources to launch, or how will they manage them.
- A function is a program or a script which runs in AWS Lambda.
- Runtime allows functions in various languages which runs on the same base execution environment.
- An event source is an AWS service, such as Amazon SNS, or a custom service.
- Lambda layers are an important distribution mechanism for libraries, custom runtimes, and other important function dependencies.

- Log stream allows you to annotate your function code with custom logging statements which helps you to analyse the execution flow and performance of your Lambda functions.
- AWS Lambda is a Platform as a Service (PaaS). It helps you to run and execute your backend code.
- AWS EC2 Is an Infrastructure as a Service (IaaS). It provides virtualized computing resources.
- Deploy and manage the apps on AWS Cloud without worrying about the infrastructure which runs those applications.
- AWS Lambda is used for running and executing your Back-end code. You can't use it to deploy an application.
- AWS Lambda helps you for the ETL process.
- The best practice of Lambda function is to use the right "timeout.
- It is not appropriate to use AWS Lambda software packages or applications which rely on calling underlying Windows RPCs
- AWS Lambda is a highly flexible tool.
- AWS Lambda tool is not suitable for small projects.
- A common event which will be triggered when you use AWS Lambda is Insert, updating and deleting data Dynamo DB table.

www.ingramcontent.com/pod-product-compliance
Lightning Source LLC
Chambersburg PA
CBHW070837070326
40690CB00009B/1582